STRONG. F

MW00344505

Rose McAleese

All rights reserved. No part of this book may be reproduced, scanned, or distributed in any printed or electronic form without permission.

Please do not participate in or encourage piracy of copyrighted materials in violation of the author's rights.

Copyright © 2011 Rose McAleese
Published: June 2012 by Litsam, Inc.

ISBN-13: 978-1-935878-06-3
ISBN-10: 1-935878-06-3
E-book ISBN:978-1-935878-07-0
LCCN: 2012934861

This is a creative work. Names and stories, fictional and factual, are rendered from the author's imagination. Any semblance to persons living or dead, or events past present or future, is entirely coincidental.

Truth is an unfolding story.

Litsam
for the books!

Published by Litsam, Inc.
Shoreline, WA U.S.A.
http://www.litsam.com

STRONG. FEMALE. CHARACTER.

When I was 18, I landed a job as an intern for a film production company. That internship quickly turned into a real job. One of the things I did there was read scripts and one of things I had to look for while reading scripts was a strong female character.

I realized pretty quickly why I was chosen for such a daunting task. I was the only girl at my job. I was surround by men who were also looking for a strong female character but weren't entirely sure what that might mean.

This elusive character had to be smart, loud but not too loud, funny but not funnier then the boys, sexy but not "slutty" and she had to be special but not cocky about it. She had to have perfect breasts, small hips, blue (no, green) eyes, tall (well, not too tall), and skinny (but not scary skinny). I was beginning to think that there is no such thing as a strong female character.

I was truly fed up with this wild unicorn chase. There was no way I was going to find this SFC. My quest was hopeless. But then it occurred to me that, outside my job, I was surrounded by strong female characters. She does exist, just usually not on paper and most def not written by a man.

During one of my many self-proclaimed downhill spirals, my mentor Daemond Arrindell said to me "Rose, someday you're going to have to face the fact that you are a really strong person."

I wondered, could this be true? Could that strong female character be trapped inside me? When I write it down it sounds so freaking corny.

The truth is I am still trying to figure it out. I recognize SFC's around me every day. They keep me balanced, earthbound, solid, and hopeful, especially when I think that maybe, on my best days, I might be one. So this collection of poems is my road map for finding her.

That mysterious unicorn.

The Strong Female Character.

First.
Feel stupid and guilty.

Then say it and forgive yourself.

(Begin.)

I want love.
I want you,
I want you so bad.

I want car
bus
rumble
roll.

I want cab fare.
I want pace
rustle

rush
timing.
I want heavy
peel
push.
I want pull.

I want bitter,
so badly.
I want smile.
I want respect.
I want status.
I want you.

I want hurry
love,
hurry.
I want naked.
I want eye contact.
I want avoidance.

I want to create
importance.
Fame, flash, notice, click
click like fame.
I want click.

I want stare.
I want long
walking.
I want curve.
Palm, creases,

hold.
I want hands.
I want better bones.

I want keep.
Bury,
deep.
Howl.
I want noise.
I want monster.

I want protection.
Soft,
slow burn.
Marriage of salt and wound.

I want milestone.
Print, paint, fill space.
Bold, big, make room.
I want ready.
Ready.

I want wild
crazy,
savage.
I want battle.
War, flesh.
Fresh.
I want before.

I want sleep.
I want wrinkle.

I want account.

Find the "I" in stupid.
Feel the guilt in want.

I want notice.
I want crave.
Value,
taste, soak,
spit.

I want birthmark.
Teeth marks.
Lasting effect.
I want moss on my tombstone.
I want after.
I want different.

I want road.

I want build.
Broke, ground.
Start.
I want up.
From bottom.
I want hammer.

I want stay.
You.
Stay.

I want free.

I want smart.
I want space.

I want nasty.
Disasters, blaze.
Fire pit, scorn.
I want ash.

I want daddy.
Dad, please.
I want praise.
I want mother,
holy possibilities.

I want this now.
I want again
and again.
I want,
I want.

I want trust,
in all you do.

Trail off.

In this event,
life.
It all depends on what you get.

FLYING ANIMALS 101

For my mother

"The gun gives you the body, not the bird"
-Henry David Thoreau

Flying Animals 101 should be taught in schools.

Because if we are going to "ground" our children
with ethics and rules,
cut them down
using fractions and wit,
we might as well give them a soaring chance
to believe
that something out there
is actually flying.

That embarrassment of wanting to stare out windows
instead of filling in spaces with lead
is okay.
There's a leap for that.

An action
in which a bird
is not aware of the ground below it,

then realizing there isn't anything missing in the world,
it jumps.

We humans don't bend our knees enough.

Crows make mocking sounds
on telephone lines,
tackling noises caught in their beaks,
they rustle their feathers
and flap up a ruckus.

Take note in their actions.
Notice how even when annoying
they got you listening,
didn't they?

Robins are bright and distracting
but push out their chests
and fly forward.
Swallows are too humble and careless
but can smell fear
and notice quick predators.
Hummingbirds are tiny yet agile,
wouldn't dare listen to a mocking bird
or a taunting foot walker.

My back has been hurting a lot lately.
Maybe it's the weight of growing up
or that my bones
now brass, not hollow,
hold more than they used to.

(Why did I ever learn about gravity)
or believe that humans cannot be held by air alone.

Flying Animals 101 would have told me
that, in fact, the pain is just my wings
begging to break free,
to grasp the flicks of a drowsy breeze
but now
stiff,
stuck,
and retreated
under a pale shell
leaving this body here
to be grounded.

SISTER COLLINS

"I am a retired Irish Catholic."

-Peter O'Toole

If I listened to you, Sister Peterson
I would never have been free.
Free
to have the free will to question
the man-hood of this thick plot
buried inside me
like a confession,
tucked in my rib cage
like cherrywood church pews.

I learned the most about what not to do in a church.
I heard more silences in Sunday school
than a lonely girl should.
But you, Sister Collins,
you looked lovely every time.
You were bright like a sweater.
You were there to mediate
the needy, sick, poor, and uneducated.
You Jesus-lover!

You,
　　being broke in many places,
give your palms a break,
slip them apart for a while.
I know you want to, Sister Collins.
Instead of praying, you wished.
You carried your ruler like a child,
never using it once.
You're too sweet to be a nun.

But please, for the Love of God!
Witness something awful
and enjoy it for the sweaty god-garbage mistake that it is.
God made that happen,
God let the good die,
and left the poor broke
and keeps evil breathing
because God meant to.
As a nun, I'll bet you have a lot to say.
A lot more to confess.

You don't speak often enough to be wrong, Sister Collins,
not true enough to be rapped like knuckles.
Speak to me.
At this rate,
you'll say more at your funeral.

Before you die:
have you ever stood in front of your mirror naked?

Sister Collins was a nun who followed Sister Peterson.
Sister Peterson was the gray sweater of the church.

The one who followed orders
in order
and never taught lies or answers,
just the God,
the God holy truth,
while Sister Collins
was trying to be a gray sweater
but underneath
she wore red.
Red lace,
a red lace bra.

I am sorry to offend,
but seeing your eyes laugh from the impolite questions I
    asked Sister Peterson gave me hope,
gave atonement meaning.
Seeing beauty was never a sin.
I prayed you would laugh one day.
Do nuns laugh, Sister Collins?

Enlighten me with its first coming:
laugh until your ribs stitch like crucifixion,
until your face pulls tight like burning flesh.
Do you remember when you stopped witnessing and
    started to believe?
When will you open the back door of the church again?

There is more out there!
You know what I am talking about:
more than the spine of a Bible.
There are lands untold,
lands where the women sweat gold

and the men break back their neck bones to look up to God;
where the devil coats his throat with honeysuckle.
Birthplace of sin, sounding so sweet.

Sister Collins,
you know I am distrusted.
I was born here,
I have prayed before
but never meant it.
But this,
all that is about to be witnessed,
is atonement
for lost times.

I am a bum,
ashamed to actually believe in the good in others.
So I left the church.
Left my miracles and blessings on the alter
right next to the letter I wrote:

Dear spaces in the bible,
You're the holiest things I could find.

BOBBY SANDS

For my father

He told me he wanted to be able to see my bones.

You fucking do this Bobby, I better be able to see your
    every splinter.

He wants to see my bones
as though he doesn't have any of his own.

I told him,
you can have my backbone once I am done with it.
I won't be needing it where I'll be going
because there's a war out there.
Whether you believe it or not.

You bastards might have the rest of this world fooled,
leaning on the crutch that this is a religious war,
that this, indeed, is no war at all
but Troubles.

That we are just "troubled",
that we Irishmen are just swine,
that we are just ungrateful savages,
the grit and grime under the Queen's fingernails,
Europe's dirty little secret.

If this is so, then abandon us.
Abandon our homes, our pubs, our schools.

You have already made every Sunday Bloody,
flogged our language from our tongues,
made us human targets.
We have learned to beckon your bullets
take your steel and knead it in our flesh.

But my death will not be by the gun.
It will be wrung from me.

Our plan is to be prison bars
spaced evenly apart,
a stand of two weeks between each man.

If one falls,
one rusts,
another replaces him.

This was our turf,
our civil rights,
our rolling hills.

This was our hunger strike.

The strike was never destructive,
never will be defined as weakness.

We were never criminals.
We are political prisoners.

You forget that your "holiness" is mad-made.
You forget that not all prisoners are of war,
not all wars have terrorists,
but all terror happens when something is neglected.

I will neglect this body.

I will vanish,
disappear right in front of your eyes.
It's called an Irish prison break.

I will become so thin, I will be able to escape like the
    light from my window.
Slowly I will evaporate.
There will be nothing left for them to occupy.

I will become Ireland's other famine.

Day 8
My lips are chipped paint.
This hunger is roaring.

Day 14
My marrow has dried up.
I am no longer producing mucus.

Week 3
My flesh is tucked, puckered,
banged around bone.

Day 28
The hunger has become a wounded fawn.
We look to each other like old friends,
betting on who will go first.

Day 46
The more I lose,
the heavier my
body
becomes.

Week 8
I've never felt this close to God before.

But no one will worship this.

This wasn't suicide.
This was murder.

My name is Bobby Sands:
you've never heard of me.

My name is Bobby Sands.
I am a father. I am not a terrorist.

My name is Bobby Sands.
I was born here; I don't know if I can say the same for you.

Day 66
My name was Bobby Sands.
Freedom is the last thing I remember craving.

TO THE CATCHER AND TO THE RYE

It's by chance,
or fate,
that a collection of words
can link,
connect and make a classic,
something either forced
or praised by the unity of many.

A thread.
A story.
An unravel.
A novel.
A boy's journey through haystacks.
A coming of age.
Passage of time
with season after season of
crimson shades to blooming buds.
All the trouble held under that cracked armor.

Boys,
depending on my age,
have either hurt,
intimidated
or fascinated me.

Whether they were crushes,
distracted lovers,
or friends.

So bold and manly,
they taste nothing of chamomile
but react like a tincture,
accidentally skilled, using
a precise measurement of doubt,
a smaller amount of humility.

Charismatic.
Idiotic.
Hell-bent.
Willing.
Careless.
Failed.
Enraged.

All my lovers, I baptize you with these names.

A conjunction of quick action and bad timing,
taunting remarks,
fireplace burning.
There's a chance you might be turned down
by your own hands.

Embarrassed to be sane
or praised
or loved
or inspired.

Holden,
you are a careful kind of silly,
searching and side-stepping, walking
like a hermit crab: a stumbled scholar.

Your creator made you of his own flesh,
maybe even a rib, a finger nail or two,
of his body.

I won't lead you on.
I don't love you.
But I wouldn't mind touching your soft spot,
your holy temple,
grace index to the lace of your jaw line,
crane neck in wonder to what you are to say next.

Holden Caulfield,
profound boy with too much age in your spindly body,
you've done this before.
You are boy.
You are troubled,
lost.
The resistance in your skin
is so romantic that it would be cruel to love you.
I would do nothing but enable you to such beautiful
    destruction.

Dizzy, desolate,
daunted by where to rest your eyes.
Which girl
will be willing to sacrifice a part of herself in your name?

In memory of you, all standards are ratified.
That you are boy,
human, all
that, that is opposite of me.
Boys,
you will break hearts.

You will taste iron in her blood.
You will fuck up.
You will ruin, then run.
You will and can cry.
You will bury your hands
or ball them like this.
You will be a leather wallet in one of your lifetimes.
You will be your own mother in another.

Boy you are stained.
Boy you are slacked.
Boy you are breathing.
Boy you are ruling.

Boy,
    you are brass.

I am learning to forgive and bless before I slander or
    crucify.

Boy.

An unintentional illusionist
awaiting words and stories
in no order,
just breaking even as well,
shifting arguments that are turned sour by our own
    stupidity.

I've battled with boy for too long now.

I know now to tread lightly and to keep all my kings
in the back row.

Ode to Something I Never Possessed

I was careless to think this was mine to keep.
That woven in between the moments there was some-
    thing tangible.
I was foolish to believe this was lasting, sealed, a
    watermark.
It was never mine to begin with,
but why does it feel so absent?

Ode to the things we cannot see:
We expect so much more presence from you.

Ode to the itch,
the one we do not scratch, that we do not show any
    attention.
Ode to the wind,
only noticed in its absence.
Ode to the laugh,
although so packed and contagious, it has no real subject.

Ode to the silence,
no matter how deafening,
still not thick enough to see.

Ode to the trust we spoke of,
such a heavy ideal, we expected something more defined
    in feature.
Ode to the promise,
filled with the breath of our lungs, we are surprised it was
    not delivered in a package.
Ode to the forgiveness,
let it linger but not be resolved.

Ode to the kiss, the spit you creased her forehead with.
See it rest on the surface; watch carefully
as it never is absorbed.

We do not own these things, so we cannot call them our
    own.

We are not our manners,
not our names, not our bruises.
We are not our hopes, our pleasures, our wants, or our
    anger.
Not our mothers, not our lovers, not our own.

We title these things, these statements,
these unforgiving unknowns,
wild possessions.

I was foolish to call you my mine,
when you do not even belong to yourself.

THE SURFACE

(This is all that I know to be true.)

The surface,
is tender color.
This is what draws them in.

1. Every inch of my body,
can't help but be touched.

I play stupid.
Pretend I am a wild child.
Present myself with the intention that I could never to be
    tamed,
but then...

my collarbone has always been a dead giveaway.

2. Finger tips,
that's all you really need to hold a good conversation with me.

3. I will hold you close,
but just for a moment.

Once I've discovered new soil,
a better balancing act,
hands that can mimic an oil spill,
I won't remember the length of your jaw line anymore.

4. No human,
but yourself,
can ruin this moment.

I don't plan to stay.

I am just casing the joint.

Looking for soft lips,
arms that can hold the mass of minutes,
hips that can sharpen my edges,
keep me on my toes.

I am not planning on making this a home.
I am not planning to smile in the morning,
because I won't be there.

I can pinpoint this feeling on a map with my eyes closed.
I can mark this moment in the name of my pleasure.

  McAleese

I find it to be freeing.
Wanting.
Thriving.
A quick fix,
something I need for the time being.

Just remember,
this isn't for you.

There are two bodies in this second.
Pressed together like lavender in a Bible,
stamped on my tongue: holy sin-stealer.

In the end,
it really could have been anyone.

5. I do plan on making eye contact.
Just not right away.

I am just keeping track of the best skin.

MATCH AND FLAME

Letter from match to flame

They told me this was a coming-of-age thing,
a rite of passage.
That this is what is supposed to happen.
But I am beginning to question the ways of the world.
Why must we both go the second you are born?

Our lifespan is too quick, not enough time to know each
    other.
First we are put under such pressure,
forced to spark.

Does this heat ever get to you?
Is this too rough for you?
Does this hurt?
Oh, love. The friction makes me so aware.

You are split from yourself and moved to wick
One that holds you longer, one that holds you tighter.
I can't help but stare and watch you go.

Hurrying up the walls,
a wedding dress made of smoke.

I watch as you linger from my tip to the ceiling.
Where do you go from here?
Are you locked in the vents of floorboards?
Do you soak the wallpaper with your sweat?
Press yourself clean to windows, head north for the valley
   up above.

Such bitter partings, my beloved.

Letter from flame to match

You are so young, weak at heart.
Made of wood,
Earth's best creation, man's worst conductor.

You are so naïve. You wish nothing more than to be their
        soot, their chalk, their ash.
Don't you see what they do with me,
what damage they make of me,
what harm I am capable of?

All you see is my smoke,
a veil fit for a funeral.
I hurry away not for the mystery but out of shame.
If only I could leave you faster.

There is no beauty in my creation.
My scream, a warning;
they should have listened to the crackle from my rush.
My throat is raspy; it's hard to breathe.

No need to sweeten this.
You are just my maker.
I met you with such disgust in mind,
arranged marriage.

I flicker out of struggle, not of dance.

POSITIONS

When he left.
I was bowled over with so much anger.
Here I was again.
Alone.

So frustrated and pissed off, I did the only rational thing
    I could think of.
Yell at the night sky.
Curse at the amber stars.

Those stupid twinkling lights,
so proud and bright.
How dare they look at me that way,
most likely mocking me,
probably snickering, too.

Some show, huh?
Did you enjoy it?
    I asked.

Neck craning so they could see all of me
melted, face smeared with tears.

What a fall that was.
What a tragic stumble,
what a failed attempt that was to love.
The trip was half the rush; the landing,
not so soft.

Of course, there was silence.
First ashamed and then followed by my own
    awkwardness.

I saw them turn towards me
so I was able to see all of them.

They replied.

"Silly girl,
You think any one of us cares if you mortals crash and burn?
You think we constantly want to be placed in constellations?
We've been doing this for years.
You think anyone cares about what we wish for
before we come tumbling down out of the comfort of this
    velvet?

"Maybe you shouldn't press your luck to so many moving
    things."

  McAleese

MASON JARS

The men who don't come home from war
leave behind women.

The crease of an elbow,
holding the weight of waiting.

Empty mason jars,
collecting dust on America's windowsill.

Contain clovers,
honey,
July's blackberry jam,
knotted kite strings,
rainwater,
thumbtacks,
curse words.

The lids of these jars
are tight,

desperate for the familiar touch of hands to loosen them.
Release them.

The sweat of loneliness drips
on such fragile flesh
and marinates the widows of today's dead.

WHY I DON'T WRITE LOVE POEMS

"People are no damn good. And men are worse."

- Charles McAleese

I have come to the conclusion that I am not made for
    love.

That feelings are tightly wound compasses,
just trying to make it home after a long night.
Romance is just a store-brand laundry detergent used to
    wash away your naïvete.

Why do we love love?
Love clearly hates us.

I don't trust men who know my middle name.
I don't trust men who can charm my father
or drink like him either.
I don't trust men who smile too big
whose best traits are all physical.
I don't trust pretty boys with nice eyes.

I don't trust guys who ask: "If you can't have children
Why do I have to wear a condom?"

First,
left me with a mouth of rusty nails and a clinic phone
     number.

One,
led me to believe I could save fish from drowning.

That man,
gave me a hammer and told me to fix my own problems.

White boy called me intimidating:
"Too much!"

Lover,
not the same shade as me,
reassured his mother, I was "just" a friend.

Boy,
told me we would work out because he didn't want
     children
but he made sure to call me a dead-end before he left.

There is a pattern.

I love like my body: Barren.

Men who say I am too strong
need to be men about it.

Handle your shit.

Make eye contact.

Speak more clearly and louder, when you are walking
    away from me.

I will use this as experience,
hold it against the next poor sucker who marches his
    pretty little face my way.
Pray for him, clipped birds. Let's hope he gets out of this
    one alive.

Alert the others that I lust like war,
know how to snap necks,
swallow nails,
and flirt like Medusa.
Be forewarned, I am a man eater
who is developing serious hunger pains.

I don't need to believe a thing you say.

You are no blacksmith, no lumberjack.
Everything you leave is made of sugar.
This will all crumble with one lick.

Maybe it's my fault.
I wear tap shoes to bed.
I like a good entrance
and hate silence.
I have a soft spot for hipbones.
I love with escape in mind.

Maybe it's my fault that I care with too many keys,
that I stain every lover with rust.
Because if I can't be beautiful,
I will make sure no one around me is either.

I am not bitter,
I am just being a man about it.
Fucking.
No kissing.
Not trapping myself in situations I can't charm my way
    out of.

I take after my mother.
I also take after winter.
I am a cold bitch.

I promise to leave quietly this time,
just a sweaty palm-print on your door handle.

Boys,
How can you not love a girl with a good exit strategy?

Ultra-Nostalgia

"And everytime somebody ask me
If I sing songs to get at women,
I say yeah."

-Frank Ocean

Dear Mr. Ocean,

I've been meaning to write you this letter. But I just
haven't found the right pen yet, the write sword to
slice this paper with, the right ink to dissect the
marrow of these memories. Haven't found the time,
between coffin-making and mapping out the direc-
tions to my temple for the next man. I've been trying
to keep busy.

My thoughts: terrible bumble bees. I am mistaking that
buzzing for a sinking melody. A song of mourning,
but I need to know, whose death we are celebrating?

I smelled the ashes of failure even before there was a fire.
I am beginning to grieve my own scars even before the
blade touches the skin.

You were always there. In the strangest of ways,

The chalk that surrounded the body at every lovecrime.

When he pulled me away from him, like a rib,
He, no Adam,
me, no Eve,
it was your song that I heard dusty in the distance,
mistaken for the second coming of Nina Simone.
When the guilt of fear crawled across my body like a
    spider's web,
it was your mumbling I heard in the spaces of my
    breathing.

Now you bury yourself so deep in these songs, you could
    call it 6 feet under.

So a girl like me, obsessed with saving decay, shouldn't be
    surprised I fell for a boy
obsessed with the undertaking of things.

Frankenstein's orchestra:
bones for fiddles, lungs as harps, elbows played in D flat.
I live in your stitches.

I am so desperate for someone to stroke the pitch out of
    me,
core out my tones.
Notice, there's arsenic in these notes.
It's sickening how close we are to death.
I am begging for someone to shake the swim from the pit
    of my stomach.

Mr. Ocean,

When you get home do you trace the body, with your left
hand, ring finger,

American like?

Do you collect the keys of every Lincoln you ever had to
pull yourself out of?

Do you ever wonder if she will walk, no, stroll back into
your room,

no, back into your life,

wearing nothing but your blood-soaked button-up,

draped across her shoulders, a painter's smock?

The Greek in her marble hips, screaming to be chipped,

the scent she carries will be seedless grapes,

all of this staged just to a muse you.

You are no heartbreak. You are no pity.

You are no one's simple.

You are no one's black suit

but your own.

We are just two pastel strings of lights, running parallel
from each other.

Maybe we will never cross paths, but there will be dirt
involved in both stories.

We may never meet.

But I'll keep playing: a tune from your soundtrack.

This feeling, this heavy, will sink soon, right?

There will be tears, I know there will be tears.

But please tell me this will dissolve, be released into
novocaine.

Frank,
I've kissed him so many times, my lips no longer belong
    to me.
I scratch my skin to erase his fingerprints.

I am trying to believe in something while holding onto
    nothing.

Please tell me this too shall pass.

Sincerely,
The women in your songs

WHITE MALE

Days I wake up
thankful for the things I am not capable of doing.

A police siren paints an echo across my window
as it passes.

This sound,
haunts,
chills,
puts me on ice.

I wake up shaking,
soaked in someone else's cold sweats,
my spine
a tightrope with too much breeze in it.

Last week I woke up smelling like a forest fire.
Yesterday I woke up tasting like salt.
But this morning

I wake up thankful for the fact that I will never give birth
to a white male.

Sun,
I apologize in advance.

I shall call you Sun,
because some days I will be the only one who knows you
    shine like one.

This world is cruel
and maybe
it's because you are in it.
But people
will tell you what you are like even before they get the
    chance to meet the rise cast behind those thin lips.

There are silver spoons stuck in the gaps of your teeth.

That is not the sunlight.
Don't let the sun play tricks on you, white boy.

You will speak with a heavy, privileged tongue.
Some days I will be the only one to understand you.

I fear you because I know better.
I fear you because I know headlines.
Hate crimes.
Frats.
Rapists.
Tally marks.
I know the South.

And I know
police academies.

I know
fire trucks.

And as my child I know you will not be putting out the
    fires but dancing among the embers and the ashes,
with a match stick in your hand, chest billowing out
    proud, like smoke.
You will be soaked in someone else's cold sweats,
my gasoline honey.

My child!
What have you done?

You will come into this world
all fists and salt,
craving ocean spray.
You will jump into shark-infested waters
because you can.
Because you want to know what it feels like to swim away
    from something bigger than you.

There is a fear growing inside me.
I buckle at the weight,
I cannot carry this on my own.

How will I sleep at night, knowing
you
will come
into this world with more power
and privilege than I.

But I will rock you to sleep while the world is
BANGING
on the door, demanding to see the monster I have
    created.

You will not be fazed by this.

Your kind can sleep through anything,
really talented at not seeing what's in front of you.
In fact, your slumber is thicker and lasts longer when
    there is white noise involved.

You will be white noise.
You will be white devil,
Motherfucker.

You will never be sunlight.
You will be smoke.
You will be privilege.
You will be great white shark.

And as your mother, I will be held responsible for all the
    repercussions of bringing gasoline honey into this world.

I apologize in advance.

There are days I am thankful for the things I am not
    capable of doing,
but years I am thankful for things I will never have to see
    him destroy.

THE CHILDREN

For Claire, my sister

If I have a daughter, she will be beautiful.
But not the kind at first glance.
Her beauty will be the type you have to really look at,
allow your eyes to adjust to.
If I have a daughter and she's anything like me,
she will bite the end of words like she's running out of
    breath.
Like she's running out of time on this planet.
She will be not be clean but well-kempt.
She will crave mint leaves when she cannot sleep,
will place tea bags over her eyes if she cries.
She may get mush-mouth or tongued-tied, but will not
    be muffled.
She will be able to break the wrists of any man who
    touches her too soon:
a trick she learned from her father.
She will have the smarts to walk away from anyone who
    tells her she's too much:
a skill she clearly developed from me.

If I have a son,
he will be marble as much as he is Irish.
He will know how to iron, cook a well-mannered meal,
    and carry like a tool belt,
not like a man, but like someone who truly cares about
    the fix of things.
If I have a son, he will be dressed to the nines.
Like his grandfather, he will have swag and fancy tucked
    in his lapel.
He will be evenly buttoned.
He will wear a watch before he knows how to tell time.
He may spit or stutter but he will never mumble.
He will love nothing like me, because he will be better at it.
He will allow himself to be tender,
wear his heart on his sleeves, even when they are rolled up,
a skill he clearly did not develop from me.

If I have children, they will not be afraid to get their
    hands dirty.
They will have broomstick spines, straight and able to
    collect their own broken.
They will love whomever they please.
They will have laughs like Christmas lights.
Their anger will come like last month's unemployment
    check: late and it won't last long.
They will have wonderful birthdays.
Their hearts will skip beats on the first day of school and
    they will have goofy grins.
They will bury the strangest things in the back yard for
    me to dig up later in life.

And I will not be mad.

I will crack a smile and roll my head back as joy giggles
    its way up my throat.
I will be happy, fulfilled, as any mother would.

If these things happen,
if these people do come to life,
it will be a miracle. A shock to us all.
There are no children.
There may not be any.
But if there comes a point, I will be ready.
They will most likely not be from my body.
But I will love them.

Oh,
how I will love them as though they were.

A WOMAN'S WILL

You want to divorce me?
You wish to
divorce me.

You silly crow,
wingspan too short of raven.
You foolish king.
If it was not for me
you would have no hunger for demise and conquer,
or crave the flesh of another.

I,
Your lady—
No chambermaid—
Rest assured in barren bed for you,
sit waiting,
past midnight's crooning moan.

Your robes,
washed daily,
by these very hands.

Stone, cold water, rinse,
make absence of any bloodshed.

I,
your wife,
clean up all your messes.

You pay no judgment in such rash decisions.
No grounds are made for your ruling on such pressing
     matters as these.

Divorce? You've wandered too far, my dear.
Coward.
I am calling you nothing but coward.
Hollow.
No backbone to aspire.
Where will you go, Sire?

Oh, Macbeth,
such childish quarrels push us back on our demand.

Who will shine your blade,
iron the wrinkles out of your halfhearted strategies?

It is the Queen who makes all the moves.

My scenarios unravel like chess.
You are a pawn.
Oh my worship,
you are just a wooden pawn.
Names of former lovers
hang over the mantelpiece that is my heart.
Men, not worthy of royals,
you are lucky not to be sacrificed.
I saw flint in your ambition,
spark of potential as my lord.

You may risk the tattling of the morning's light,
fold the night sky into your fist,
but I planted the seedling that will grow into our
    Kingdom.

I know that the women here back their husbands,
are victims, naïve and God-smacked,
but I play shadow,
stitched close to your heels.

Because I,
Lady Macbeth,
make every dagger a happy one.

You will set out on this task as my husband.
You will be rubies,
feast,
throne,
King of Scotland.

I will be by your side,
cinched tightly.

Bash the ridiculous notions of failure.
One must steal if one is not given.
I vow, no sleep will be lost over this.

And I know, from experience,
all blood can easily be washed away.

BLACKBERRY PICKING

For Jackie & Ericka

Late August came with wet skin, rain, and heavy sun.
This being the last times of many firsts for us,
we plucked the glossy berry from the stem.
You told me not to eat the first one, savor it for later's
    pie.
We envied the berries' color, like the thickness of wine,
leaving stains on our own skin, tongues: the lust of picking.
Our mother's good bowls ran with juice and using our
    skirts as baskets,
we searched and gathered even when the tins were full.

While picking we talked about boys.
The rain ran down our skin, August showers forgave us.
The thorns of lovers, past, present, or distant, peppered
our skin as we plucked the darkest of the fruit.
The nectar was sticky sweet, our conversation never
    turned sour.
Unturned berries in the bowls; red, green, hard ones
    left behind.

The lust in these berries is jealous of you, the fullness of
    your hips.
Purple blooms across our hands and lips as we gather
beautiful, rich fruit, with August's sun divided between
    you too.
Summer's blood. Soaked into our flesh.

THANK YOU

I would like to thank so many people. I want to thank
the family I was born into and the family I grew into
and the awesome and generous people who have sup-
ported me as a poet, writer, and all-around goofball.
There are so many to name and think of.

My Family:

Mom — You are my best friend, my rock, my mother,
and thank goodness, my editor. I am sorry for giving
you so much sass as a kid.

Dad — You taught me to be proud of who I am and
where I come from. You taught me style, manners,
and most of all how to charm the pants off of people.

Claire — Even though we fight and bicker like old mar-
ried people, I truly respect you. And it's not because
you are my sister; it's because I love you no matter
what. Your name is still the first word I ever learned.
I will always look up to you even though you are
shorter than me.

My YouthSpeaks Seattle Family

You guys have helped me and watched me grow. You
have kept me sane. A special thanks to Daemond,
Hollis, Chris, Angel, Denise, Tara, Karen, Maddie,

Lily, Kyle, and Matt for being my mentors and my extended family.

Trio Calling For A Quest

Jackie & Ericka — You have seen me through almost everything: car accidents, heartbreak, and bad style choices, as well as being part of some of the best times of my life. Thank you for telling me to stop whining and go do something about it.

Special Thanks

Mary —You are one of my first and dearest poetry friends. You've always been there for me with a birthday card and jar of Nutella in hand. You're the Maya to my Ela.

Jackson— For being like an uncle to me. For always e-mailing me poems and goofy YouTube videos.

Maya & Ela — Thank you for being supportive friends, soul sisters, surrogate parents, and tough competitors. If you two had a son, we all know he would be my dream guy.

Easier Than Google: Rose's Bio

© Janae Jones

Rose McAleese is a poet and a filmmaker who was born on Halloween night in Seattle, where she was delivered by a doctor in a giant spider costume, which, so far, has pretty much set the tone for the rest of her life.

She began writing poetry before she actually knew how to write, filling dozens of notebooks with her indecipherable scrawl. Her penmanship and spelling eventually improved and she was named Individual Youth Slam Poet in 2007 and 2008, and was a member of the Seattle Youth Slam Poetry Team that competed at Brave New Voices National Poetry Slams in 2007, 2008, and 2009. She also competed on the University of Washington poetry team at the 2010 College Unions Poetry Slam Invitational, where she was nominated Best Female Poet. She was a member of the 2011 Seattle Adult Poetry Slam team and was named "Rookie of the Year," an honor she found both flattering and funny. In 2012 she represented Seattle at the Women of the World Poetry Slam.

She works as a freelance writer, editor and director in her hometown of Seattle. In her spare time, she occupies herself by considering her next move and working on her tan. Neither project seems to be working out as planned.

CPSIA information can be obtained at www.ICGtesting.com
Printed in the USA
BVOW01s2325160614

356466BV00001B/2/P